CW01270773

Follow That Dream
The Business Owners Guide to Setting and Achieving Goals

Peter Messervy

FOLLOW THAT DREAM
The Business Owners Guide to Setting and Achieving Goals

ISBN-13: 978-1530045075

Published by
10-10-10 Publishing
1-9225 Leslie St.
Richmond Hill
Ontario, Canada
L4B 3H6

For information about special discounts for bulk purchases,
please contact 10-10-10 Publishing at 1-888-504-6257

Printed in the United States of America

Contents

Foreword ix

Preface xi

Chapter 1: Dare to Dream 1

Chapter 2: Find Your Dream 13

Chapter 3: Clarify Your Dream 27

Chapter 4: Set a Path to Your Dream 35

Chapter 5: Focus on Your Dream 49

Chapter 6: Capture Your Dream 63

Chapter 7: Putting it All Together 79

I dedicate this book to my thousands of clients and students who have provided me with honest feedback and ideas that have helped me grow and improve over the years.

I hope, like me, you never stop learning.

"Our deepest fear is not that we are inadequate.
Our deepest fear is that we are powerful beyond measure.
It is our light, not our darkness that most frightens us.
We ask ourselves, Who am I to be brilliant, gorgeous, talented,
fabulous?
Actually, who are you not to be?
You are a child of God.
Your playing small does not serve the world.
There is nothing enlightened about shrinking so that other people
won't feel insecure around you.
We are all meant to shine, as children do.
We were born to make manifest the glory of God that is within us.
It's not just in some of us; it's in everyone.
And as we let our own light shine, we unconsciously give other
people permission to do the same.
As we are liberated from our own fear, our presence automatically
liberates others."

Marianne Williamson, a spiritual teacher, author and lecturer

Foreword

Have you ever considered how your present life is contributing to your long-term dreams? Like most people you are probably far too focused on the present moment, with all its activities, pressures, and deadlines, to spend too much time on your future.

Have you ever wished you had time to make changes and improve your situation? Have you ever thought that it was time to make serious changes, but never knew how to get started? Again, if you are like most people you are responding to unexpected events rather than a steady planned path. You may be unaware whether or not all your efforts and energy are even contributing to your long-term goals.

Your life is probably filled with activities, obligations and commitments that have nothing to do with your goals or your dreams. You may be spending your life running faster and faster trying to keep up, and at the same time falling further and further away from living that extraordinary life about which you are dreaming.

Peter has faced many challenges in his business and personal life, and has emerged a victor through hard work and persistence. When you hear him speak you know there is something different. Something resonates, what he is saying is true, even though you may not have heard it expressed in that way before. He has spent many years on the front lines of business growth and development. He has worked with many types of business from sole practitioners to Fortune 500 corporations. His coaching and training has created many raving fans, as his testimonials prove. In reading this book you will no doubt feel the depth of his experience.

Today there is massive waste in business. A waste of time, money, and human energy, at a huge cost to our current and future economy. A major cause is the unknowing application of effort to the wrong things. Peter's vision is that every individual in business can make incremental improvements by learning how to find the right path using their own innate strengths, and follow it to a successful outcome.

In this book you will find very simple ideas, guidelines and suggestions that you can follow to empower you to transform your business. Start applying this now and create positive lasting change in your business and your life. I'm sure there are many ideas and suggestions in this book that will resonate with you.

Raymond Aaron
Leading Transformational Success Mentor
New York Times Best-Selling Author

Preface

I have been teaching business and systems subjects in corporations and universities for many years. Early in the process I learned that teaching on its own almost never had a lasting effect in an organisation. What was required was fairly extensive follow-up to create and nurture any change that was sought. Thus my business coaching developed as a way to ensure positive lasting change and secure the return on investment for the training.

In my coaching activity, the first steps almost always involve some form of goal-setting. In the same way as teaching, one discussion or one work session was never enough. Even when the client was, at that moment, enthusiastic and dedicated. To have any lasting effect, regular review and reinforcement was required.

I found I was repeating a fairly standard process over and over to almost all my clients, and I was frequently asked if I had this written down so people could do some of their own reinforcing. So here it is; I have finally written it down.

There are many publications about goal-setting, and I didn't want to cover the same ground without something that had additional value. In my years of practical experience in teaching and coaching I have crafted my own method. I have studied the human brain research as it relates to business and leadership behaviour, and incorporated that knowledge into the process.

This book is my humble attempt to gather and present enough useful information to help individuals in business and leadership positions. By reading this book, I hope you will develop an understanding of the challenges in the pursuit of goals and how to overcome them. I hope you will then have the confidence and willingness to set challenging goals with an expectation of a successful outcome.

I wish you good fortune in following your dream.

Peter Messervy

Chapter 1: Dare to Dream
The Power of Goal-setting

- What is a goal?
- Why should you think about goal-setting?
- Why should you set goals?
- What is the impact of goal-setting?
- A story of commitment
- Where does the power come from?
- The *Path to Success* model
- How can you avoid failure?

What is a goal?

Following a dream is a process of envisioning a desired future and purposely setting out to achieve it by creating one or more goals to get you there.

A goal is a specific future outcome that you can envision clearly, and are willing to expend some effort and resources to achieve.

Why should you think about goal-setting?

There is a particular statement made in almost every book and course about goal-setting. So I would not like to be the one who didn't include it. It has many variations, but one of my favourites is the one by Darren Hardy in his book *The Compound Effect:*

"You only see, experience, and get what you look for. If you don't know what to look for, you certainly won't get it."

Quite simply, people with clear goals achieve more in life or business than those without. There is a lot of research and empirical data supporting this statement, which can be found online and in the many research papers available.

Do you want your future to unfold by design or by chance? The trouble with chance is that it can go either way for you.

If you are satisfied with your current life and circumstances and there is nothing more you wish for, this book is probably not for you.

If you prefer to live a life directed totally by the events and external influences that encroach on you every day, this book is probably not for you.

If you are a person who has set goals before and failed to achieve them; if you have lost your faith in goal-setting and no longer believe in goal-setting, this book is definitely for you.

If you have never bothered to set goals and you are interested in how goal-setting works, this book is definitely for you.

Why should you set goals?

To deliberately define the future you choose, so that you can take the appropriate action to reach it in the most efficient way. This is known as The Law of Intention. Living without goals is allowing circumstances and other people to determine your direction and your outcomes. Life is then a direct result of what you tolerate. You can choose your outcome and plan a path to reach it. Or you can allow random events and the influence and needs of others to choose it for you.

It is vital for your business to have clear goals. This sets your desired destination, and the direction of the plans and actions that will expend your resources. You are going to commit time and other resources to getting to your destination, so it is important that it is chosen with careful thought. It would be a pity if you didn't like it when you arrived.

Many people I deal with as a coach are functioning well below their capability. It is usually because they are engrossed in their daily activities and have no specific trigger to step back and check their purpose and direction.

People are often working hard on the wrong things for their long-term purpose. They may feel satisfied in the short term because something is being achieved. However, if the achievement is not directly contributing to a long-term goal, there will be an underlying dissatisfaction or frustration that the desired outcome does not seem to be getting any closer.

- A goal provides an anchor point to direct your planning.
- Your plan provides a framework to guide your actions.
- The right actions are the building blocks to the success of your business.
- Knowing that you are progressing in the right direction greatly increases your confidence and motivation.

What is the impact of goal-setting?

Setting goals affects you in the following ways:
1. Focused attention – this helps direct your efforts towards goal-related activities, and away from irrelevant activities.

2. Motivation – properly aligned goals greatly increase your motivation in carrying out the tasks.
3. Performance – pursuing goals helps you organise your time and resources.
4. Self-confidence – you begin to recognise your own ability and competence as you move along the path you have set.
5. Overcoming obstacles – when pursuing a goal, you are more likely to find ways to overcome obstacles.
6. Changed behaviour – Goals can help you change your behaviour.
7. Enhanced self-development – When pursuing goals, you are much more motivated to undertake any necessary learning.

A Story of Commitment

Many years ago I had a friend who had a dream. His dream was to build a sailing boat, live aboard, and make a living by chartering to small parties and taking them where they wanted to go. This friend –I wall call him Les –was an immigrant and refugee who started with no resources. Les was married and had no children. The story occurs in Canada.

Everything Les did in his life was focused entirely on achieving his dream. Let me share with you how he did this.

He started with a job, of course, in construction. He saved his money and learned how to build houses. He eventually acquired an old property and upgraded it while he lived in it and then sold it for a considerable profit. He found a piece of land and built a new house, that he lived in while building it and then sold it.

There are some remarkable behaviours that Les exhibited while he was doing this. He refused to acquire anything in the way of material possessions that were not explicitly related to his dream or to the work required to get there. He saved every penny and lived as simply as possible. When he and his wife lived in the new house he was building, they camped in the garage and cooked on a camping stove so the house would not be soiled in any way. He did all the work himself with his own hands and with owned or rented tools. He did have friends who helped from time to time with the heavy lifting. I counted myself among his friends.

What is even more remarkable is that his wife totally engaged with his dream and happily went along with all these restrictions in her life.

Eventually he had enough money to have a 40 foot steel hull built to his specifications. When this was done he placed it in a covered boat yard and proceeded to build every remaining part of the boat himself. At this point he camped in or beside the boat and his wife stayed with her mother nearby.

During this time Les needed a lot of lead for the keel. He acquired it by going around hospitals and collecting the lead containers from the radio-active isotopes used in radiography. This was a disposal problem that hospitals usually had to pay for. He did it for no charge and got his lead for free. It took many months. This is one example of the many creative ways Les used to acquire what he needed.

Eventually the boat was launched and then completed. Les and his wife moved aboard and sailed off into the sunset (actually in this case it was the sunrise).

The whole process took about ten years. Les did not have written goals and plans. He had no formal training, just shear dedication and a single-minded approach that allowed for no distractions.

I do not know or have heard of anyone else who could do this. There are probably others but I expect they are extremely rare.

Most of us need a less rigorous and more structured approach to achieving our own goals. If you are like Les, don't bother to read on. If you are like me and need more help, continue reading.

Where does the power come from?

Humans have consistently proved they can achieve amazing results in every type of endeavour, sometimes overcoming incredible barriers. It is often stated that if you can think of it, you can make it happen. So you should be able to achieve your goals. But it does require something more from you.

There are obviously some things that one individual cannot expect to achieve. It would be unreasonable for a 70-year old man to hope to be selected for the Chelsea football team. (Who knows? Perhaps in the next century.) There are some things that cannot reasonably be done by one individual.

The power comes firstly from the absolute belief that you can do it. Your brain is a powerful ally if you use it properly. Your subconscious mind tries to direct what your conscious mind focuses on. This is hardwired into our brain. Without instruction, our subconscious mind directs us to do the safest thing possible to avoid threat, pain, and discomfort. If we are trying to achieve something that is outside our comfort zone or is a risk to our status quo, then our subconscious mind will try to distract us provide us with rational reason not to do certain things.

Our undirected subconscious is a barrier to anything that requires us to change something. To turn this barrier into an ally we must take some action to direct it. We do this by providing ongoing training to our subconscious mind in the following manner:

- A clearly envisioned dream with a visual reference
- Clearly written goals that we read repetitively
- Some form of pattern that the brain can get used to and adopt
- Frequently renewed resolve

These devices will be incorporated into the various parts of this book.

The Path To Success Model

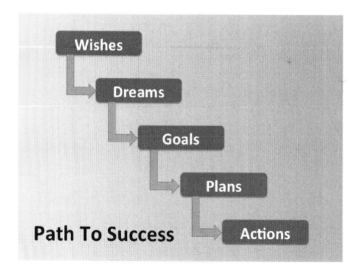

Wishes can actually be a barrier to achievement. Unlike the wishes of a child, unencumbered by the failures in life, adult wishes often imply a sense of envy or implied belief that it is not likely. For example: *"I wish I could do that," "I wish I had that job,"* or *"I wish my luck was better."* These statements root in the brain as something belonging to someone else, not us.

Think about these statements instead: *"I must learn how to do that," "I must go after that job for myself,"* or *"I must do something about my situation."* This is telling the brain that I plan to take action, so pay attention brain.

Dreams, in this book, refer to a visualisation of the wish coming true. What does that future look like? This visualisation is very important because it is creating a clear picture in your mind of what you are going for. You need to turn your wishes into dreams and, in those dreams, create a clear picture of what your future will look like with that achievement. That picture becomes rooted in your subconscious mind.

Be very careful here not to glamourise the picture and ignore any less desirable aspects. If you do that you may be disappointed when you arrive. You must want the dream with all its ramifications.

"I loved this house when I bought it but I didn't realise how much work it would take to maintain it."

"I so wanted to live here but I miss my friends and family as I don't see them enough any more."

"I always wanted to run a larger business but now I don't get to do the work I enjoy anymore."

Make sure when you visualise *your* dream, that you think of every impact that it will have on your life. In your visualisation, you may find the dream is not what you really wanted after all. Find another one instead.

Goals are the heart of the process and the rules and mechanics of goal-setting will be explored throughout this book.

Plans are the mechanisms for making sure you expend your efforts and resources on the right things and avoid distractions and wrong paths.

Actions are the tasks and activities you continuously undertake to get you to your goal and realise your dream.

How Can You Avoid Failure?

To avoid failure it is useful to understand why other people have failed to achieve their goals. Here are some of the reasons that could cause you to fail:

Lack of confidence in your ability to sustain the necessary effort
If you suffer from this, I hope that by reading this book, you will find the confidence you need. The techniques I show you will help you believe in yourself and eliminate the elements in your life that cause doubt.

The goals become boring after a while because they are not so exciting
If your goals are boring it is for one of two reasons. One, they are too small and not challenging enough. We need a challenge to sustain our interest over time. The other reason is the goal does not truly align with our passion. I will show you how to avoid that problem in chapter 2.

Current events and distractions keep you from working towards your goals
Most people have set goals at some time and most people have had some failures. It requires a number of factors to make it work, and this book attempts to provide you with the tools and techniques to give you the best chance of success.

You have tried setting goals before and it never worked for you
This can give you a built-in skepticism. Your past failures predispose your brain to believing it doesn't work for you. Successful people ignore this self-limitation and try again.

You weren't clear enough about your vision so the goals become fuzzy in time
If your goals are not thought out, clearly stated, it is hard to plan effectively and to identify the right tasks. This leads to uncertainty and lack of confidence in the steps you are taking. Clearly defining your goals is described in chapter 3.

You don't renew your commitment regularly so focus fades
If your goals are not regularly reviewed they will naturally decline in in your focus. It is perfectly normal brain behaviour to replace older items of interest with newer ones. You will find an understanding of this and some techniques to deal with it in later chapters.

And here's the big one:

Not understanding how your brain handles goals, commitment and distractions
Your brain will help you achieve your goals but it will also help you abandon them. You need to understand the triggers and responses to be able to avoid an easy path to abandonment vs. holding on to a commitment. I deal with these concepts in greater detail in the latter chapters of this book.

Of course, I can't guarantee that you won't fail. But I can tell you how to minimise the probability of failure. It would be logical to start by tackling the reasons for failure listed above. The most promising way to avoid failure is to adopt the right mindset and take action. Follow a process and know when to adapt it.

Chapter 2: Find Your Dream
How to Identify the Right Goals

- What type of goal?
- What do you really want?
- Clarify your dreams
- Discover your goals
- Don't sell yourself short
- Make your goals congruent
- How deep are your required changes?
- The final test

What Type of Goal?

Before you go any further you should consider what type of goal you are setting. Different types require different thinking, and different levels of commitment.

Consider the following possibilities:

To achieve your long-term dream is your big goal. This may take several years so it is very important to choose it well and plan it well. It will impact a major portion of your daily life for a long time to come.

To acquire something you don't already have can be short or long term. It can be large or small. Some examples are a particular house or car, a vacation to a particular location, a new office for your business.

To achieve something you have not yet achieved can also be long or short term, large or small. Some examples are to win a medal in a sport, to get a promotion, to win a business award.

To do something beyond your usual routine is likely to be a something special outside the main activities of your life such as climb Mount Everest, take a space flight, visit Antarctica, build a model railway, learn to paint.

To become someone you have not been is often a life-changing goal that requires you to change something about yourself, and is probably one of the most difficult goals to achieve. It could be the typical losing weight goal, or changing your profession, trade, or skillset.

To remove a problem or difficulty is usually a short-term goal to remove some obstacle or difficulty that can prevent progress toward your destination. It can also be an isolated issue that you want to resolve.

To establish a clear direction towards an outcome is most likely an intermediate goal to set the stage and prepare yourself for bigger changes you want to make.

What Do You Really Want?

If you have not done this before, start with a wish list. Think about things you have wished for, or the things you currently wish for, and make a list – your wish list. I already mentioned that wishes alone can be mental barriers. When you feel a wish coming on, examine it carefully. Ask yourself "What if ...?"

What if that wish came true? Consider all the implications surrounding the granting of the wish. Envision the results and decide if it really is a dream you want to come true. The tools I show you later in this chapter will help with that decision.

Example wish list:
- I wish I could get a raise.
- I wish I had a bigger house.
- I wish I could afford a new car.
- I wish I could lose weight.
- I wish I could increase my sales.
- I wish I could grow my business.
- I wish I could win the lottery (well NO, not that one).

A worksheet for your wish list is included in the bonus package that you can download from the web site. See chapter 7, Bonus Package.

Now consider your dream list.

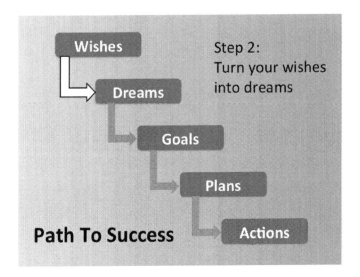

Think carefully about each wish and evaluate it. Turning a wish into a dream means culling the list to the things that are truly important to you. The list doesn't have to be long; in fact it may only have one big wish if you like. This could be a brainstorming exercise on your own or with family or business partners.

Your dreams have to be things you have some control over and can influence the outcome. Dreaming of things totally outside your control (such as winning the lottery) or the laws of physics is a waste of thought energy.

Now the "What if ...?" part. What if it came true? Examine all the consequences of that fulfillment and see if you can accept them, preferably like them. For example if you wished for a raise, would that mean more working hours, or doing a job you didn't really like?

A worksheet for your dream list is included in the bonus package that you can download from the web site. See chapter 7, Bonus Package.

Clarify Your Dreams

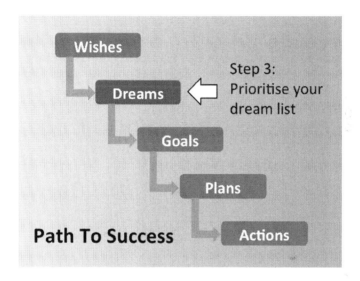

Take your dream list and prioritise it and/or categorise it. If you have a long list, you might group it into the types of goals that are listed above or into short, medium, and long-term fulfillment.

Your list or each category should then be prioritised based on relative value to you.

Some examples of dreams might be:
• Become a millionaire
• Travel across Asia

- Be on the British Olympic cycling team
- Be the number one supplier of my product
- Retire to a villa in Southern Spain

I am focusing on business goals in this book, but if you are a business owner, it can be difficult to completely separate business goals from personal goals. After all, you probably run a business in order to provide the income and lifestyle of your personal dreams. Success in your business can be a subjective definition. It depends what you want from your business.

You may be satisfied with a sole proprietorship that makes enough profit to maintain your current and comfortable lifestyle. But what if you can't work for some reason, like sickness or injury? What if you current market dries up? Do you know what actions to take to continue to survive?

You may be satisfied with a small business with a small number of employees and not want the challenges of a larger organisation. But what if key employees leave you? What if you can't find good employees?

You may decide that you can trust your ability to deal with any situation at the time, and you don't need to think about future problems.

So think about these questions:
- Do you have enough income or capital to sustain you through a mishap, a downturn, or a disaster?
- Could you shift direction if the market changed?
- Could you take a vacation without slowing the business or dropping income?
- When you retire will you have enough to sustain the lifestyle you would like to have?

Successful goal-setting depends on having clarity about your ultimate destination.

Now for the Dreams to Goals bit ...

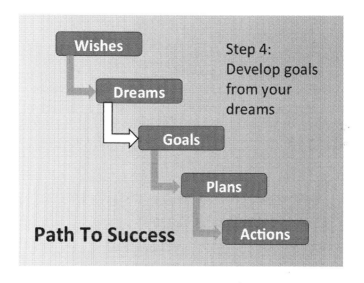

Goals are not randomly plucked from the air; they must come from some perceived need or want. Having a clear outcome in mind is the starting position for your goal-setting. There are certainly different sizes and types of goals but they should all contribute to getting to your ultimate destination. Knowing your ultimate destination allows you to be clear about your needs and wants, and set meaningful milestones along the way.

Three basic levels of need or want:

1. *Problems that Need Solving*
   This is often a short-term goal to remove some obstacle or

difficulty that can prevent progress toward your destination. It can also be an isolated issue that you want to resolve.

2. *Opportunities for improvement*
   Typically this is a medium-term goal for something that is needed or desired along the journey to your destination. Sometimes it is an unexpected addition to your plans.

3. *Personal Dreams, Desires*
   This is a longer-term goal that gets you to your final destination or to the major milestones along the way.

The first item would appear to be the most urgent and the third the least urgent.

However, in terms of importance (as opposed to urgency) the order is reversed. There is a risk, therefore, that the longer-term goals may be postponed or even ignored. This is perhaps one of the most common reasons the "big" goals fail.

I have already defined a goal as a precise future outcome that you are willing to expend some effort and resources to achieve. If the dream is large or the path to it is complex, then there may be more than one goal to achieve the fulfillment of the dream.

Don't Sell Yourself Short

For many people, setting large goals can seem audacious (who am I to be so successful?). So we are often reluctant to set our goals too large. Should we dare to set our sights so high?

The answer is absolutely yes, to do anything less is a dis-service to ourselves. Goals that are too small and with little challenge become self-limiting.

How Big?

Nelson Mandela once said:
"There is no passion found in playing small – in settling for a life that is less than the one you are capable of living."

When you don't find the goal meaningful you tend to put off the action. Goals that are specific and appear difficult to achieve tend to increase the likelihood of achievement more than goals that are not. You know a goal is big enough when it is both exciting and scary.

Make Your Goals Congruent

A goal must be congruent with your beliefs and values. It should incorporate three key criteria to be able to survive the distractions and disturbances of life.

- Skills – what am I good at?
- Value – what serves the world?
- Passion – what do I love doing?

1. You must have the skills necessary to achieve the outcome. The skills can be something you already have or have yet to acquire. Alternatively your plans may be to use the skills of others, as long as you or your business have or can acquire them.

2. The outcome must be something you value, or in the case of your business, something your customers value and will pay for. Otherwise the result will be meaningless.

3. You must be passionate about the journey and the outcome, otherwise you will soon be distracted and bored.

If you have only one or two of the three, the goal will almost certainly fail.

Passion alone is worthless without action to back it up.
Skill alone is boring and tedious.
Value alone is just a pipe dream.

- Passion and skill without value is self-serving and results in a worthless outcome.
- Passion and value without the skill will soon expose you as a fraud.
- Skill that produces a valuable outcome without the passion will not hold your focus and commitment.

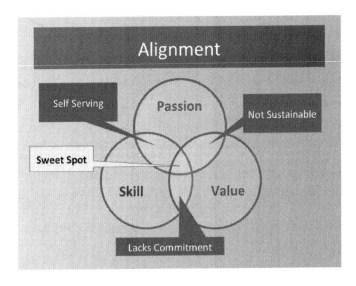

How Deep Are Your Required Changes?

It seems reasonable to assume that your goal is to reach an outcome that is different from your present condition. This means that something has to change. So working to achieve a goal is going to be (and should be) outside your comfort zone and will create some stress. Goals are rarely achieved without cost.

I use a concept referred to as the *Identity Iceberg*. The iceberg diagram below illustrates the different levels that make up who you are. The deeper the level, the greater the effort required change.

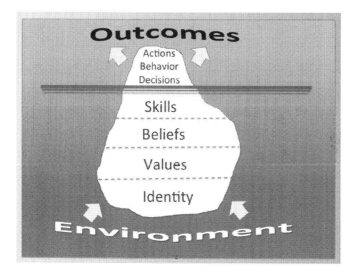

Starting from the bottom, your identity is made up from your upbringing and your environment. It contributes to the determination of your values.

Your values are what you feel about things. Values determine your perception of honesty, ethics, social responsibility, and materialism. These are influenced by your environment and upbringing but developed by your life experiences and the company you keep.

Your beliefs are the things that you think you know to be true. I say think, because often they turn out not to be true. Beliefs can be a problem because they may limit your ability to evolve. Beliefs come from direct or vicarious experience.

Skills are the competencies and capabilities you acquire in life through training, learning, or experience. Your skills are often constrained by your beliefs. If you believe you are no good at something, you never will be.

Above the waterline, your actions, behaviours, and decisions are what people can see of you and what create your current outcomes. These are shaped by everything below. If you try to change any of these without also changing something deeper, the change is unlikely to last.

In order to change, you start from the top down. Here is a simple formula to help you determine your changes:

Abilities + Actions = Outcomes

The abilities you currently have and the actions you have taken (or not taken) have resulted in your present condition. If you want different outcomes you will need to change something.

Every one of these three can be changed. Change is applied by working from the top down in the iceberg.

First define the outcomes you want. These are your dreams and goals. Then you identify what you have to do (the actions) to get there. Finally, who do you need to be (your abilities) to be able to successfully perform the actions?

As you determine who you need to be, you are redefining your iceberg model.

As you are going to bring about a change, you will change your actions, you will change the decisions you make, and you will probably alter your behaviour in some way.

As you work your way back down the iceberg model, you next identify the skills and competencies required of the person you need to be. You may have some or all of them and you may have to acquire those that are missing. This becomes part of your goal planning.

The skills and behaviours need to align with your beliefs. If you are trying to develop a skill and you always believed you couldn't then it will not work. But YOU CAN CHANGE YOUR BELIEFS. Ask yourself what kind of beliefs the person with your target identity would hold. There are techniques to help you change your beliefs. Some of them will be covered in the next chapters.

Your values are much more difficult to change. This is what you *feel* about everything. If you can't feel good about the changes, then you should rethink your goals. If the goals are really important, you can examine your values and prioritise those that support your developing identity.

If you change the upper levels, then your identity will change to some degree. One of the biggest factors affecting you is your environment. Are you in an environment that matches the identity of the person you are becoming?

The final test.

All change is possible, but the deeper the change affects you, the greater the effort required. Evaluate your goals to make sure that they pass the three criteria, you know what you need to change, and you are willing to commit to the necessary effort.

Once this is done you are ready to move on to the mechanics and the mindset to make it all happen.

A worksheet to help you validate your goals is included in the bonus package that you can download from the web site. See chapter 7, Bonus Package.

Chapter 3: Clarify Your Dream
How to Define Your Goals for Successful Achievement

- Know your "Why"
- Do some imagineering
- Clarify your goals
- Make your goals SMART
- Write your goals down!
- Evaluate your goals
- Goal-setting mistakes

Know Your "WHY"

You have identified your dream and one or more goals. It is very important for you to consider why they are important to you. Your next step is to consider each dream or goal and write down your WHY. Why do you want this?

- Is it to do something you love and believe in?
- Is it to improve your lifestyle in some way?
- Is it to achieve status?
- Is it to prove something to yourself?

Be careful with this. If you write down "make more money," consider that money itself has no real value, it is what you want to do with it. So ask yourself how you will use the money. That is your real why.

If you are looking to impress others in some way, this is typically not of real value to you. Look for what you really want, not what you think others might want you to do.

You should know exactly why you want it. The stronger the reasons, the stronger the goal. Also consider what's at stake and what are the consequences of not achieving it.

Do Some Imagineering (Envisioning)

Yes, I know it isn't a real word, but you must admit it is descriptive. By now you have gone through the goal-setting process in the previous chapter. You have one or more dreams and one or more goals to work on. Go back to the dream level and generate a vision of your dream by imagining the finished scenario, which involves visualising every possible aspect.

Warning! This is where many people fail. They skip this step because they think it too trivial or even a bit too much like play. I urge you to carry out this process. Even if you have to hide yourself away from prying eyes and do it in secret. But I hope you don't have to go that far.

There are different techniques for doing this.

One is a meditation-like process. Sit back close your eyes and put yourself into your future. Use all your senses; imagine sights, smells, even the feel of things as you touch them. Make the imagery as complete as possible.

For example, you might envision a business office at the top of an important building, or a small building of your own. Imagining what it would look like, what colour is on the walls, what is the furnishing is like, what pictures are on the walls, smell the leather on your executive chair, smell the coffee brewing in your espresso machine, and so on. Fill in all the details.

One of the values of doing this is that it creates a sense of pleasure or excitement that confirms your vision. Sometimes it has the opposite effect and you realise that it wasn't what you wanted after all. It is an effective decision making tool to imagine each possible scenario in detail, to put yourself in the picture, and let your feelings guide you to the best choices.

Another technique is to create what is called a dream board. You do this by selecting a large panel of some kind; it could be a piece of cardboard or a corkboard. Over a period of time, keep a look out for materials that remind of your dream. If we still consider the office above, look for pictures of office interiors that appeal to you, cut them out and put them on your board. Do the same for furniture, fabrics, coffee machine, and so on. If you want a particular car, get a picture of it. If you want a certain kind of house, get some pictures.

You can put anything you like on your dream board; pictures, words, phrases, anything that reminds you of your dream components.

This may seem to you to be unnecessary at the moment; you are excited about your dream and it is fresh in your mind. But as time passes, ideas and images fade and you might lose track of your earlier thoughts. The dream board is a powerful reminder that keeps your brain stimulated with your dream.

Keep the dream board visible in a place where you can see it every day. You can add and subtract items too, if you find suitable improvements.

Clarify Your Goals

Through imagineering you have confirmed your excitement over the outcome. Your brain is now in creative mode, so make good use of that. Revisit your goals now and write them out in detail.

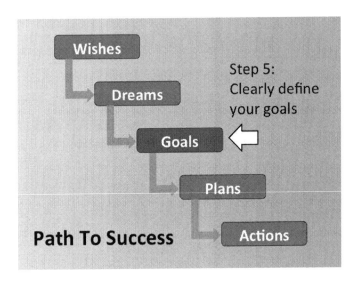

The goal statement should be inspirational. You will need to be re-inspired as time passes.

Make Your Goals "SMART"

You can download a free SMART worksheet for capturing your goals.

SMART is a well-known acronym used in planning and goal-setting. It establishes 5 basic criteria considered essential in setting a goal.

Specific—your goals must identify exactly what you want to accomplish in as much specificity as you can muster. Be as specific as you possibly can, envision as much detail as possible. The more complete the picture, the more committed you become to the goal.

Poor Example: "Take a vacation."
Good Example: "Spend three weeks this summer touring the Greek Islands."

Measurable—as the old adage says, "you can't manage what you can't measure." Try to quantify the result as much as possible. Find something you can measure. This enables you to know unequivocally when you have reached the goal.
Poor Example: "Earn more this year than last."
Good Example: "Earn £/$5,000 more this year than last."

Actionable—every goal should start with an action verb (e.g., "quit," "run," "finish," "eliminate," etc.) rather than a to-be verb (e.g., "am," "be," "have," etc.)

Poor Example: "Be more consistent in blogging."
Good Example: "Write two blog posts per week."

Realistic—A good goal should stretch you, but you have to apply common sense. Over your comfort zone is good but not to the level that over-stresses you.

Poor Example: "Qualify for the PGA Tour."
Good Example: "Lower my golf handicap by four strokes this season."

Time-constrained—every goal needs a date associated with it. A goal without a date is just a dream. Make sure that every goal ends with a by when date.

Poor Example: Lose 20 pounds.
Good Example: Lose 20 pounds by December 31st.

A SMART worksheet for your goals is included in the bonus package that you can download from the web site. See chapter 7, Bonus Package.

Write Your Goals Down!

Write goals down – The act of writing them down forces more explicit statements of intent. Daydreaming about your goals does not help you to reach them. When writing goals, the process helps you make sure you have all the elements. This is the first of several commitments you will have to make to yourself to reach your goal.

Research shows that those who write their goals down accomplish significantly more than those who do not.

A comprehensive study of Harvard University MBA graduates was conducted in 1979 and 1989 with the following results.

1979 – How many had written goals?
    3% had goals written down (Group A)
    13% had goals not written down (Group B)
    84% had no goals (Group C)

1989 – Average earnings.
    Group B earnings were twice those of group C
    Group A earnings were ten times more than group C

Evaluate your goals

As you go through this process, each of the steps above provides you with a mechanism to evaluate and test your reaction to what you have created. You may find you change your mind along the way, or discard a goal after thinking about it. This is quite normal. It is better to abandon or rewrite goals that don't meet your needs at this stage than put in effort and discover you have wasted time and resources.

The way you decide if a goal is worth achieving is through planning and analysis of the elements of the goal.

Goal-setting Mistakes

Here are the most common mistakes I see people make when it comes to goal-setting:

- **Not written down.** The Harvard study above should be sufficient to convince you to write them down. Naturally when written they must be reviewed regularly. I mentioned before how details fade in time. You must be able to recapture the enthusiasm when you need to.
- **Not viewed in broad context.** Setting business goals or career goals without considering the impact on all aspects of your life can produce unpleasant surprises. For complete fulfillment you need goals that have a positive effect on all aspects of your life.
- **Not making SMART goals.** This is already discussed in the section above.
- **Not challenging enough.** Goals that are easy to achieve can become boring and are often abandoned for lack of interest. Set goals outside your comfort zone and stretch yourself a

little. Don't underestimate yourself and set your goals too low.

- **The due date is too soft.** Set your completion date so that it is realistic but creates some pressure on you to get it done. If you don't do this you are likely to find distractions or procrastinate until it is too late to hit the target.
- **Too many goals.** Don't create too many. You are likely to have more than one goal, but avoid having more than you can stay focused on within your lifestyle. Conventional wisdom suggests no more than 10.
- **Not accessible and regularly viewed.** Your goals must be kept somewhere you can review them regularly. Ideally they are visible to you at some suitable place in your habitat.
- **Insufficiently detailed action plans.** If you don't have clear actions and next-steps, it is too easy to leave out critical activities and lose direction.
- **Dependent on chance events.** Your goals should not rely on events that are outside your area of control or influence and may or may not happen. Certainly luck can play a part in limiting your obstacles, but not in your success.
- **Not reviewing your progress.** Regularly review your goals and your progress. This is vital for retaining focus and avoiding distractions.

Chapter 4: Set a Path to Your Dream
How Plan a Successful Outcome

- Goals to plans
- Why planning is important
- Horizon planning
- Commit to action
- Discovering the activities
- Keeping your plan fresh

The Goals to Plans activity in the Path to Success Model

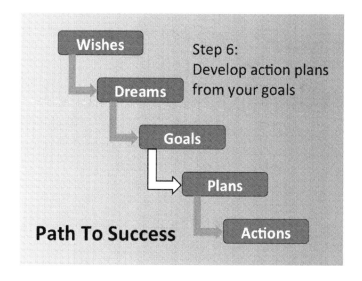

Identify the steps it will take to get there, the resources needed, and the obstacles you will encounter. Make the steps small enough to have regular achievements. Small successes along the way do wonders for morale and commitment. Conversely, working for long periods with no measurement to show progress is almost always demotivating.

Why Planning is Important

Why you should plan?
* Understand the work to be done
* Make sure the work can be done in your expected time frame
* Manage expectations
* Evaluate performance and progress
* Predict resource requirements
* Manage change
* Measure success
* Create a visible reference

A plan is a collection of artifacts that define different aspects of the project that are necessary to guide you to a successful outcome. The plan should answer the following questions:

* **What** must be done?
* **Who** will do it?
* **When** must it be done?
* **How** will it be done?
* **How** long will it take?
* **How** much will it cost?
* What is needed to get it done?

I am often asked why bother to plan when so much is uncertain.

The fact is that life is always uncertain. The simplest plan for taking a train journey can be derailed (excuse the pun) by train delays and other adventures along the way. That wouldn't stop you planning which train to catch, from which station, and to what destination. You might well consider the uncertainties (risks) and include some contingency in your planning. I am sure you wouldn't start out walking in the hope of finding a station, not knowing if it is on the right route or when the trains run from it.

The plan is a framework to guide you, not a rigid set of directions. Plans almost always change along the way, but that does not alter the value of the plan. The planning process should include the following:

Identify areas of uncertainty
Keep the plan at high level when uncertain
Plan in detail only those things that are known
Make assumptions when necessary
Use horizon planning

Horizon Planning

The term Horizon Planning is based on the idea that you can only see as far as your horizon. Everything beyond that is speculation or hearsay. That means you plan in detail for the things you can see and you plan at higher levels (less detail) for the things you can't.

Short-term goals may not need this as they probably fit within your horizon. Longer-term goals, however, should make use of this technique. The reason is that you should not waste time and energy working out details for activities that have lower probability of occurring. Conditions further into the future are more likely to have changed by the time you get there. This does not negate the value of planning as it is still important to have a framework to focus your efforts.

Start the process with your dream and long-term big goal. Fulfillment may be several years out. The goal has already been established and described if you have followed the steps in the preceding chapters. So you can plot your timeline.

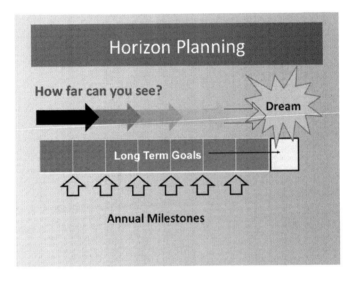

Breaking things down into manageable chunks is a great help. So it is useful if you can provide annual milestones along the way. These are intermediate achievements on the way to the goal. They do not have to be precise at this stage but should give a reasonable and logical progression to fulfillment of the goal.

Once you have done this you can shorten your vision to the end of the first year. This milestone should be a more accurate prediction of where you should be at that time. You can put more detail into your planning for the coming year. This should be as much detail as you can come up with but identifying only the completion of tasks (deliverables), not the detailed activities. I call these deliverables objectives.

These two steps are your strategic planning process.

With the one-year plan in hand, break it down into 4 quarters. Take one quarter and identify all the activities necessary to achieve the quarterly objectives. The activities should be fully detailed. This is your tactical planning process.

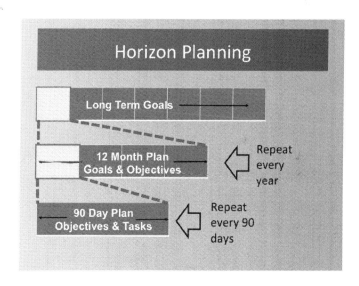

Commit to Action

Now for a most important step. Take all the activities and plot them into your calendar. This calendar is often referred to as your *Default Calendar*, because it includes all your planned activities, not just your appointments with other people. In other words, when you don't have appointments with others you have a default appointment with yourself to perform the planned activities.

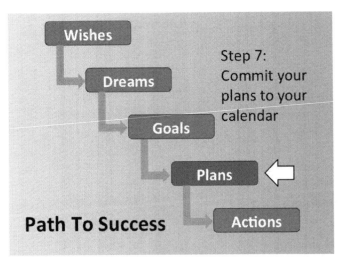

There are some conditions you should consider:

- The activity must have a time frame – duration and completion date
- The activity must fit in with all your other obligations and plans
- The activity must treated just like any other appointment you make, you must expect to do it in the time slot planned in your calendar

- The activity should be kept to short durations where possible
- If the activity spans more than one day, allocate time slots in each day
- Spread the activities as evenly as possible over the 90 days

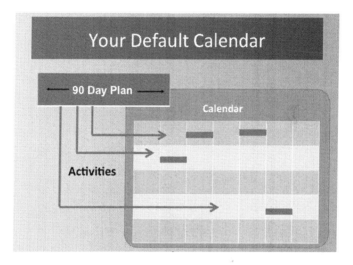

The next section explores a technique for discovering all the activities

I realise that unplanned events come up and you may have to move something. Each time there is a time conflict you make a decision about priorities. Attending to a customer probably ranks more important than anything else. When you decide to move an activity, make sure you place it somewhere; do NOT put it aside for later consideration. Treat it just as you would if it were an important appointment with a person to be rescheduled. If you don't follow this with some discipline, the plan quickly becomes obsolete and therefore useless. This is where many failures in goal achievement occur.

Discovering the Activities

An effective way to work out all the activities and deliverables is to start with the big picture and then steadily decompose it into smaller and smaller chunks until you have reached a level of small simple activities with relatively short time frames.

You could write a list, but a list is a left-brain activity and you are less likely to spot gaps and errors. A graphical approach is a right brain activity and focuses your conceptual thinking. When I do this for myself or my clients, I use a flip chart or white board and sticky notes.

If, for example, your dream was to grow your engineering business so you could sell it and retire, it might look like this:

> ### *Grow the business to a £1 million turnover in five years and sell it for £5 million*

This would probably involve a few goals such as:
- Develop a production team to handle the increased workload
- Create a marketing and sales strategy to increase the number of customers and sales
- Develop a social media presence and build a community of potential customers and employees.

I am going to take the second goal – creating a marketing and sales strategy. Naturally the goal statement would be properly developed as a SMART goal. It would take some background work to make sure it fulfilled all the SMART requirements. Here's how it might look:

> ## *Create a marketing and sales strategy to increase the sales volume from £200K to £5M by the end of July 20XX.*

Here's how to proceed:

1. **Start by writing out the big goal** and sticking it at the top of the page or board. I am going to call this big goal the *vision*.

2. **Identify the intermediate goals** that are needed to get the vision completed. Write each one on a separate sticky note and place them just below the vision. Each intermediate goal can stand alone as it delivers something complete and useful in its own right.

The goals might include:
- Goal 1: Create a marketing plan
- Goal 2: Design and create the marketing materials and scripts
- Goal 3: Execute and measure a cycle of marketing methods
- Goal 4 ...

3. **For each of the intermediate goals,** identify the key deliverables or milestones. I am going to call these *objectives*. Write each one on a separate sticky note and place them on the chart.

If I take the intermediate goal "Create a Marketing Plan" I would break this into the deliverables necessary to build the marketing plan.

Some of the deliverables would be:
- Research marketing plan structures and content and select a model
- Create a list of the components of the plan
- Develop content of the plan

4. **For each deliverable/objective,** identify all the activities necessary to get it done.

For developing the content of the plan, here are some of the activities:
- Create a list of the key customer benefits of our services
- Determine the ideal target market
- Define the target customer(s)
- Identify the different marketing methods to be tried

These are examples and the lists are incomplete but they are just to give you a sense of the process.

The chart should look something like this:

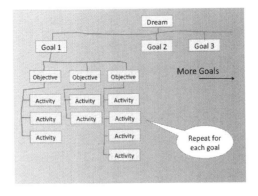

It doesn't have to be all done in one session or one day, you can spread it out and tackle one area at a time. Based, of course, on your overall time frame.

Example of Dream, Goals, and Objectives, and tasks

Dream: To own a successful, profitable baking business.

Goals
Goals can stand alone and deliver something of value and complete in their own right.

- Develop a new an exciting cake recipe
- Set up a baking business ??
- Learn marketing

Objectives
Objectives are like milestones along the way. They are not independently useful but necessary to support one or more goals.

- Set up a baker's shop
- Register a limited liability company
- Create an attractive web site

Activities
Activities are discrete packages of work required to complete the objectives.
- Find and lease a premise
- Select and acquire baking ovens and tools
- Select and acquire display cases

These activities become the activities in you default calendar.

A worksheet for your detailed planning is included in the bonus package that you can download from the web site. See chapter 7, Bonus Package.

Keeping Your Plan Fresh

As you progress and your horizon unfolds, you should add the relevant details to the plan. If there are changes to be made, the plan should be updated.

At the end of every 90-day plan, or preferably near the end, you must complete the detailed planning for the next 90 days. At the same time review the mid-term plan to see if any deliverables have changed.

As each one-year term nears its end, review the whole plan and set out the one-year mid-term plan.

I have created a habit for planning that I have described below and I strongly recommend you do something similar. It takes me very little time and it ensures that I am always focused on the right things.

At the end of every work-day, I do the following:
- Review my default calendar for the next day's scheduled activities and appointments.
- Update the default calendar with any notes, activities or changes I identified during the day.
- Create a short to-do list for any must do items for the next day, which includes phone calls and emails I identified during the day.
- Review my default calendar for the current week to make sure I am prepared or will prepare for what's coming.

- Review my next two or three weeks to make sure I am comfortable with the longer-term schedule and I won't have any surprises or rushed deadlines.

At the beginning of every work-day I do the following:
- Recheck my calendar and to-do list.
- Look at my goals and projects to remind myself of my purpose.

During the workday I do the following:
- Make a note of any calls or emails I decide I need to make as they are discovered – today, tomorrow and beyond.
- Respond to unexpected events by making scheduling decisions and adjusting my calendar as necessary.

I make sure I have time for making calls, reading emails, travel between locations or meetings, and breaks.

This does not take very much time and allows me to focus solely on the moment during the day without a nagging feeling that I might have overlooked something. Of course, I am not perfect and I sometimes do overlook something, and I frequently under or over-estimate time and effort required. Practice enables me to build in sufficient contingency to cover most inaccuracies.

I strongly recommend that you design and implement something along these lines. Once you have it working you will not want to ever work without it, I am sure.

Chapter 5: Focus on Your Dream
How to ensure your continued commitment

- Using Your Brain
- Brain Health
- Your goal seeking mechanism
- The power of positive thinking
- Building your confidence and self-esteem
- The fear of commitment
- Overcoming your upper limit

Get Started on the Action

Now that you have it in your calendar, you know when you are going to take action for each of the planned activities. At this point I want to take an excursion into your brain. You should understand how it works in a goal-setting context, and how to make the best use of it.

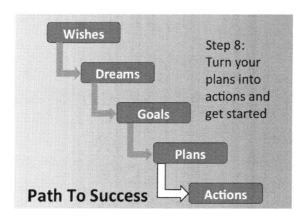

Using Your Brain

The initial effort of setting the goals is over and you are into the activities. This is where failure often occurs. How do you maintain the enthusiasm and energy? How do you keep the dream alive? The answer is right there in your own brain. Your brain can be a powerful ally or a serious barrier. And you can train it.

Before you use any tool, you should understand how it works. Whilst the brain is extremely complex, there are some basic concepts that will assist you in making the best use of it in your goal-setting.

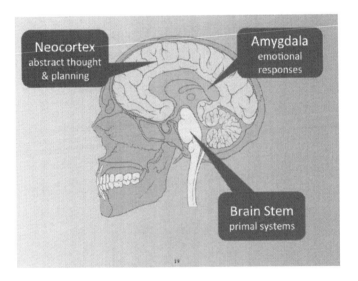

The diagram illustrates the three areas of the brain that are involved in the goal seeking processes. To be able to train your brain you need to know what factors affect these areas and the impact on your feelings and performance.

Limbic System		Rational Brain
Brain Stem	**Amygdala**	**Neocortex**
Vital Functions: - Blood pressure - Heart rate - Breathing - Hunger - Digestion Sleep & waking Arousal & alertness Freeze, fight or flight response	Emotional Responses: - Joy - Sadness - Disgust Behavioural Responses - Risks - Aggression Body temperature Pleasure, reward, motivation	Abstract Thought Willpower & inhibition Planning & organisation Ideas & imagination Language & learning Problem solving & analysis

Our brain is hardwired to react to uncertainty and pending change with fear. It is our built-in defense mechanism, honed over millions of years. The amygdala reacts emotionally, the brain stem assumes control, and the neocortex is out of the picture. Without rational thinking in play, the brain is not able to make rational, objective decisions. The greater the degree of uncertainty, the greater the innate fear, and the decisions become more irrational and erratic.

Some people have learned to override this primal reaction and force a shift back to rational thinking. It is a learned skill founded on your Emotional Intelligence.

As uncertainty is based on lack of information, the more information you can acquire, the less the uncertainty, obviously. Fear is an emotional response to an expectation of something happening in the future that is not yet real. Once aware of this natural brain activity, it is possible to see fear as a perception, not a reality. Then you can set it aside and engage the rational brain to perform an objective analysis.

Positive thoughts are an effective way to subdue the limbic system from trying to take over, and allow the rational brain to do its job. So, when you recognise the fear response you can identify it as irrational thoughts and quickly focus on something positive. Remember that you are dealing with thoughts that speculate on your future, so fear is totally irrational. This naturally does not apply to a real threat that you need to avert now. People who are good at this have a small library of positive thoughts or scenarios that they can jump to when this situation arises.

Whenever you are faced with uncertainty it is a useful exercise to identify and separate the things that are known and the things that are not known. This helps frame the level of uncertainty with clear boundaries. This is a technique used extensively in risk management. Another useful idea is to identify what you can control vs. what is outside your control.

Finally, understand that you can never predict every outcome. So when you have finished all the rational analysis, trust your gut. Our instincts have also been honed over millions of years and we should learn when to listen to them. If you are wrong, learn from it and move on. Going forward and making mistakes is a natural part of growth. Standing still is to atrophy.

Brain Health

It is beyond my intended scope of this book to go into brain health details. There are many worthy publications on this subject. So this is just a quick summary of the key factors in brain health. Pay attention to these if you want to get the most out of this amazing tool.

- Natural light
- Sufficient sleep
- Physical health and fitness
- Good nutrition
- Water
- Social interaction
- Rest from distractions
- Regular breaks

Many years ago I reached a point that I suspect is the same for many people. I felt overwhelmed, working too many hours, not sleeping too well, and feeling tired most of the time. I also found I was slowing down physically. One day I had to run for a bus and when I got on it, I was breathing hard, feeling pain in my chest and unable to speak. That was my wake up call. I used to be very fit; what on earth was I becoming?

I decided to take time for exercise out of my day. A simple decision, but here's what happened. I joined a local squash club and started to play regularly. The club was close by and I could play during the day if I wanted to. Making an appointment to play with someone made sure I would turn up. Very quickly I improved my squash skills and became enthusiastic. I steadily improved my levels of play and ended playing in regional tournaments.

It would seem that I would have had to reduce my work-load. Surprisingly, the opposite happened. I felt so fit and energised that I found myself doing more work in less time. In other words, my physical health improved my mental health and my efficiency. I was also enjoying my squash games and getting pleasure that extended to feeling good throughout my day, which also boosted my effectiveness.

I gained all the other fitness benefits as well, but the big surprise was that I was enjoying myself, sleeping really well, feeling positive all the time and getting much more done in my business. Yes, I took sometimes two or three hours out of my day but the return on the time invested was amazing.

Your Goal Seeking Mechanism

You actually have an automatic goal seeking mechanism built into your brain. Its know as your Reticular Activating System (RAS). The job of the RAS is to bring relevant information to your attention (your conscious mind) and filter out the irrelevant.

Imaging sitting in a noisy restaurant with a few friends. There is a lot of input to your senses. Literally thousands of pieces of information. Sounds of voices and background clatter, smells of food and possibly perfumes and colognes, multitudes of sights in masses of minute detail, the physical feel of things like your napkin, chair, and so on.

Your brain is receiving all this but cannot pass it all to your conscious mind. It filters out most of the information and only processes what you appear to consider important. You can direct your attention filter to focus on one or two items. 7 to 9 current items is considered to be the maximum your conscious mind can hold on to at one time.

You may be concentrating on your associate's conversation and ignoring everything else. Then someone nearby mentions your name or the name of someone you know and instantly your mind is fully focused on that conversation.

How this works for your goal-setting is that you can programme your RAS.

When you built a dream board you were visualising your goals. When you wrote out clear definitions you were visualising your goals. It is the visualisation process that trains your RAS to pay attention to things relevant to your goal. Whenever you revisit your dreamboard or goal definitions you are reinforcing the RAS, and it does need reinforcing regularly or the focus will fade beneath the weight or more recent instructions.

If you keep thinking of your goals in a positive way and avoid thinking negative thoughts about them, you are enlisting your most powerful ally in achieving them.

We need to create a very specific image of what we want in our conscious mind. This is passed to our subconscious mind. The RAS will then bring to our attention any relevant information and attempt to suppress the things which are not relevant and could be distractions.

A vital consideration is that the RAS will not work if we are trying to set goals that are not congruent with our beliefs and self-image.

The Power of Positive Thinking

From time to time we all find ourselves in stressful moments or reacting to a negative situation. During this time we often feel overwhelmed, confused, and pessimistic. When you experience this it tends to generate negative thoughts.

Negative thoughts waste your time and energy, and interfere with your concentration. In this mode you are less likely to make sound decisions and stay focused. Like it or not, you become inefficient and even careless in your activities.

Negative thoughts generate negative feelings and negative feelings generate negative thoughts.

If something negative happens to you, it will cause you to feel unhappy, which in turn will make you think of other negative things that have happened to you.
This can become an unending cycle, each reinforcing the other.

If you are anticipating something you don't like or fear, it will create stress. Stress will cause you to think about other things you fear and raise your anxiety. Your anxiety and negative thoughts are reinforcing each other.

This becomes an unending cycle unless something happens to block it.

You can wait for something good to happen while wallowing in your misery or anxiety, or you can create a change yourself.

If thoughts and feelings are so closely connected, then force yourself to change your thoughts. People use different techniques for this, such as gentle meditation to create calmness, getting angry with themselves and basically yelling at themselves – "come on, GET OVER THIS!"

Changing your thoughts means changing your perspective:
• What would I think about this if I were in my positive mood?
• How would (someone positive that I know) think about this?
• What would my friend/partner/coach say to me about this?
• What other options are there?

- What if I had to take the opposite opinion in a debate?
- What is the worst that could happen?
- I am smart enough to handle this.

This is a good time to go back and read all the positive and exciting things you put in your dreams and goals. But be careful not to do this when you are still in the negative mode, as it may initiate negative thoughts about your goals. So change your mood first.

Building Your Confidence and Self-Esteem

Self-confidence is tied to your belief in your abilities and how you feel about yourself. Self-esteem is how well you think you live up to your values.

If you think about the beginning chapters on setting your dreams and goals, both self-confidence and self-esteem may have had an impact on your choices. Either can be a self-limiting control.

Here are some things you can do to boost your confidence.

Plan a successful outcome. Ask yourself how you would behave if you were totally self-confident. Imagine the successful scenario and rehearse it your mind. This is a mental practice for the real action to follow. It is used by athletes when competing and it presets your brain to believing it will be successful.

Be willing to adapt. If a particular approach is not working for you, make changes. Don't feel you must stick rigidly to a plan if it's no longer right. But don't just make random changes or abandon plans without good reason.

Don't let fear paralyse you. Fear is anticipating something negative in the future. Something that may never happen, or may not have as big an impact as you imagine. Analyse your fear, examine the worst case scenario and understand it. Then do what you can to minimise the risk. But do *something*.

"Every time you think the problem is 'out there', that very thought is the problem."
Stephen Covey

Don't let mistakes derail you. You cannot avoid making mistakes; everyone does it all the time. Some are bigger than others, some are more visible than others. But we all make them all the time. Learn from them and get over it. Leave them behind.

Balance positives and negatives. Don't just think about mistakes but concentrate on successes and celebrate them. Give yourself a pat on the back.

I had a client who was running a business, providing much of the household income and raising a teenager. One day she was feeling very stressed and told me the following tale.

"I am working long hours, we are not making enough money, my husband is grumbling at my lack of attention to him, my daughter is acting up because I am not around enough and presenting me with all kinds of demands. The business is having a slow spell and I need to spend the time there, but I feel guilty but I have to bring in my share of the income and make sure the business survives."

I happened to know her circumstances well enough to redirect her thinking. Here is the gist of how I responded:

"You need to turn that around and look at it from the other side. You have done an amazing job building a business from scratch to where it is in just one year. You have a partner who may be a bit of a pain sometimes, as partners often are, but he is tremendously supportive and does much of the housework and chores, and he loves you very much He would do anything for you. You have a wonderful daughter who is doing well at her studies and living your values, as well as being a typical annoying and difficult teenager. You have some good staff that are loyal and work hard. So you are having a few challenges and you have proven quite capable of dealing with. Think about your positives."

It worked for her.

Here are some things to help your self-esteem.

Don't expect perfection. Always do the best you can but understand that perfection is an improbable and useless pursuit. Measure your achievement and be satisfied you have done all you can within reason.

Stifle your internal critic. Part of your brain is always critiquing your actions. It is a natural learning instinct but it can be overpowering and produce negative thinking if you are not careful.

Ignore your external critics. Beware of people who tell you it can't be done or you are not capable. It is never true unless there are some real physical limitations. But if you are not careful you can come to believe it. Especially if it's people who think they know you well and may care about you. Only you can decide what can and cannot be done.

I refer you to a famous quote by Henry Ford:

"If you think you can do a thing or think you can't do a thing, you're right."

The Fear of Commitment

The resistance to commitment is something I come across often with my clients. I hear it stated in many ways; here are some of them:

- The time is not quite right
- I just need to finish this [task]
- I am waiting for [something to happen]
- There is too much going on at the moment
- I tried this before and it didn't work too well
- I don't have the resources at the moment

There are many variations on these and you probably have one or two of your own. Well, here are some realities to think about:

- You can always find a reason why the timing isn't right if you work at it
- There will always be something you're waiting for
- If you are busy now, you will always be busy
- The fact that something didn't work out in the past doesn't mean you should abandon it. Most successful people failed at least once before succeeding
- You don't need much in the way of resources to get started

You can always find a reason to put off starting. Sometimes it may be a very valid reason, but usually it is a fear of committing driven by a fear of failure. You can start by recognising that this is a natural emotional reaction, usually about some deep-rooted fears around confidence and fear of failure. The way to deal with this is to distance yourself from the emotions and look objectively at your intentions.

Step away from the negative feelings and reconnect with the outcomes of the goals. Imagine the successful outcome and generate the positive emotions around that. By doing this you can be far more objective in balancing the two sides to see if you have a real issue.

The most effective thing you can do is to take action. Overcome the hesitation and just get started. Taking action triggers everything.

"The moment one definitely commits oneself, then providence moves too. All sorts of things occur to help one that would not otherwise have occurred."
W. H. Murrey, mountain climber

If you think you have a legitimate reason not to commit, then clarify the reason. You can either look for an alternative plan or you can incorporate the overcoming of the barrier into your goal planning. They key here is action; find some way to commit. If you can't do that you will not be successful.

Overcoming Your Upper Limit

When you experience success, you have undergone a change in lifestyle in some way. Humans don't like change, especially if it's into unknown territory. Your brain will actually try to persuade you to return to your previous level. It acts like a kind of thermostat trying to hold you in place. This can generate negative thoughts about your success (or planned future success), and you can sabotage your own ambitions.

This is why some of my clients start out fearing any more success and arguing that they are "happy" where they are. With coaching, of course, they soon overcome this and happily move forward, raising their success bar.

Chapter 6: Capture Your Dream
How to Stay On the Right Path

- Sustain the Action
- Set the right habits
- Deal with distractions
- Make enough time
- Don't feel overwhelmed
- Regular affirmation
- What if you get stuck?
- When the plan has to change
- Monitor progress
- After You Get There

Sustain the Action

This is without a doubt the most difficult part because it requires mental stamina for the long haul. You have to be able to stay committed to your planned actions in spite of your moods, setbacks and competing priorities. As I mentioned before, this is where most people give up.

The psychology and neuroscience on this subject is a constantly evolving knowledge base and there is a massive amount of material available. I have collected some key concepts that I believe will help you manage your continued commitment and action.

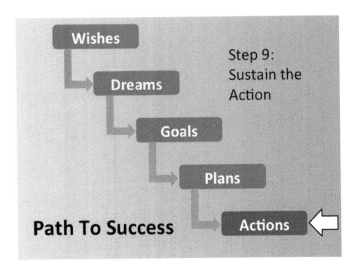

Set the Right Habits

"We are what we repeatedly do." - Aristotle

A habit is *"An acquired mode of behaviour that has become nearly or completely involuntary."* – Merriam-Webster. Two key words are *acquired* and *involuntary*.

If you acquired it you can discard it. The trouble is that if it's involuntary it requires considerable effort to discard or change it. But it can be done.

Habits are formed by doing something repetitively and over time. It is completely involuntary; your brain does it automatically as a method of conserving thought energy. There is no consideration whether it is a good or bad habit. You can consciously choose to change habits; what it takes is practice and repetition. There are no shortcuts. The greater the intensity of your effort, the stronger the habit.

We are not born with habits, we learn them. According to psychological studies, 95% of our adult thoughts and actions are a result of learned habit. Habits are essential in our daily routine, and a good thing because it means we can run our routine mundane daily tasks on autopilot. Thus freeing our attention to focus on more important things.

A habit has three parts:
1. Cue – the rigger that initiates the routine
2. Routine – the activity you perform somewhat mindlessly
3. Reward – the desired result

Example1:
Cue - Your flow is interrupted by a phone call, which causes a negative response and you feel stressed
Routine – You go and get a coffee and a donut
Reward – You reduce the stress and feel more positive energy again

Pay attention to when you experience the cue, and instead of a coffee and donut, you might do some stretching or go for a short walk. The idea is to respond to the cue with a different routine to achieve the same reward. You may have to try a few things to find out which routing works best for you.

Example 2:
Cue - A partner or associate criticises something you did and you flare up in anger
Routine – You become defensive and respond with criticism of the other person
Reward – you feel satisfied

In this case, on the cue, change the routine to something more positive like pause and evaluate, perhaps thank them for their input (preferably not sarcastically).

Earlier I wrote about having a clear understanding of *why* you want something. Your *why* (the reward) is the key; it is the strength of your *why* that overcomes obstacles and resistance.

Deal With Distractions

If you can avoid distractions, you are better able to concentrate, which frees up your working memory. Therefore you can focus more effectively on the task at hand.

We are easily distracted. Our brain seems to be wired that way. If something becomes boring, tedious, or too long, we yearn for distractions and may seize any opportunity. If on the other hand we are engaged with our task and *in flow*, the opposite is true; we will resent an intrusion on our concentration. This is where your self-discipline and brain training come in handy.

There are two kinds of distractions, external and internal. The external distractions come from other people, our communication devices, and events around us. Internal distractions arise from our brain wandering around random thoughts and worries. Worry and mood can affect our ability to deal with all distractions.

We tend to favour instant gratification over long-term results. So doing something that will give us pleasure now is preferable to doing something that has benefits sometime in the future. Even if the instant gratification results in an overall loss. This is why so few people with heart attacks are willing to forego current pleasures in spite of the risks. So watch out for the temptation to put aside the important stuff for the easier or more interesting stuff "so I can get it out of the way." This is an insidious form of procrastination.

We are constantly being distracted by people, events, and circumstances around us, every moment of our day. If there is an emotional response to the distractions, we may behave contrary to our own interests. Our daily juggling of priorities means it is easy to find an excuse not to do something. Two of our innate needs are to seek approval and to please other people. This makes us susceptible to respond to a request from someone, even if it is inconvenient or we don't really want to do it. A very useful time management skill is to know how to say no without giving offense. Of course, there are interruptions from family and other important people that we either don't want to say no to, or feel the consequences justify concession. So if you find yourself overburdened in this manner, evaluate the consequences, decide if it's important to you, then accept or decline with appropriate courtesy.

Make Enough Time

How many of you feel you don't have enough time to do things you need to do? I can tell you that it's all in your mind, and you can change how your mind perceives your time. You will never FIND time for anything, you have to MAKE it.

When we are under pressure, our imagination ventures into the future and usually finds the worst case. It makes all our future tasks look bigger and scarier that they really are.

Stephen Covey and others have used a well-known time management diagram to help guide your use of time.

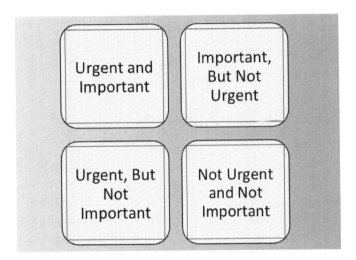

Your aim is to spend as much time as possible in the "Important But Not Urgent" quadrant. These are your planned activities. Using your *Default Diary* discussed in the planning chapter is a great help with this.

The bottom two quadrants are to be avoided as much as possible. The bottom right quadrant should be eliminated altogether. These activities are likely to be mundane routine tasks that can often be delegated or rejected.

The upper left quadrant is usually for unexpected events outside your planned routine but necessary. Try to control these as much as you can and delegate if possible.

Watch out for activities that are important to someone else but not you.

Today we are hooked into a big nagging world trying to persuade us to do things we probably don't really want to do.

Unfortunately we are hard wired to desire love, seek approval, and appreciation. Our childhood habit of permission and approval that is really hard to break. So when we are faced with an intrusion, we become stressed because our "people pleasing" instincts drag us along paths we don't want to be on.

If we are not careful we can end up scurrying around trying to win the approval of others.

Now don't confuse pleasing with serving. Serving is something you do when want to provide a service of some kind to people, on your terms rather than responding to pressures and demands.

The most effective time makers:
- Know how to say NO without giving offense.
- Know how to ignore irrelevant interruptions and distractions.
- Make choices and take action instead of procrastinating.
- Block negative thoughts and get on with it.

Managing how you spend your time is about making choices. If you are not happy with the result, you are not doing it right.

Planning and thinking ahead are important, but if you spend too much time worrying about the future you might miss creating it. The here and now is the only place where you can influence the future and create the one you want.

I accept that there are unexpected events and situations you didn't plan for and still have to deal with. Fate may deal the cards you have but it's your choice how you play them. You will be amazed at what you can do when you make time a non-issue.

Don't Feel Overwhelmed

How many of you sometimes feel overwhelmed? Let me explain something that I learned that was of great value to me. It's an illusion. That overwhelmed feeling is created by your brain when it is faced with multiple choices under a time pressure.

Situations themselves (even dramatic ones) don't cause feelings. The brain generates feelings because it always tries to interpret the situation and build a story around it. The less clarity you have about the situation, the greater the perceived risk and the heavier the story. The overwhelmed feeling is created by your thoughts about a situation, not the situation itself.

If you think about a rainy day, some people think how gloomy it is and how they feel cooped up, while others think how refreshing it feels and how it's good for the garden. It's not the rain that causes the feeling, it's the believed story that your brain creates about it.

It was pointed out to me a long time ago, that when you are faced with too many things to do, it is a failure to choose that's the problem. If we choose something and take action, then the overwhelmed feeling goes away.

So, whenever I am faced with a bunch of things in front of me to be done, I accept that I can't do them all at once, so I pause, review my real feelings about them, choose one and go for it. I have found this to be the most time liberating lesson I have ever learned.

Regular Affirmation

When you are initially identifying your dreams and goals, your interest is high and your excitement is at a peak. You find yourself full of energy and enthusiasm. It feels like it can't be diminished. Unfortunately, as time goes by the schedules and pressure of the current day push aside long-term thinking. Your brain automatically puts the newer issues above the older ones. Over time the bottom of the pile will fade into oblivion.

If this continues unchecked, you will gradually set aside activity on your goals and eventually even forget all about them. Until something or someone suddenly reminds you and it jumps to the forefront again, although probably less intense and generating less commitment. After all, you've got by so far not worrying about it.

The way to prevent this sad situation is to regularly re-affirm your commitment.

This is where the dream board and the visible plans prove most valuable. If you create the habit of briefly revisiting your goals and dreams and consciously repeating them to yourself, you will build stronger and stronger commitment that will survive the daily pressures.

Keep your dreams and goals visible where you can easily see them every day. Affirm your commitment at least once a day on a predetermined and habitual schedule.

What If You Get Stuck?

When I am designing something, whether it's a training course or a coaching program, I often find the flow of ideas for solutions dries up. This also happens when I am writing a book or a paper. My strategy is simple and it always works (eventually). I prime my brain with all the relevant data that I am able to identify and then stop thinking about it and do something else. The something else could be a different task, a walk along the riverside, a cycle ride, or even a night's sleep. It doesn't matter as long as it is something unrelated to the task. I get a kind of feeling about it when I am ready to come back to the task. I start work and the ideas flow like magic. Sometimes it's all the necessary ideas, sometimes only a few. But always forward progress.

I have been doing this for many years. Today neuroscience has determined that it is a measurable brain process. Consciously attempting to find ideas is a limited neo-cortex activity that uses your library of knowledge and experience. But this may not fit the situation. The conscious mind is now a barrier to free thinking and problem solving as it focuses on what you already know and locks you into a way of thinking. By taking a break you are allowing the subconscious mind to work on the problem. Which it can do better and faster than we can think consciously.

So when you feel stuck, change tasks for a while or take a break. Put the activity aside for a while and don't try to think about it. Then go back to it later and see what happens. You may need two or three attempts. In my own experience, I firmly believe the subconscious mind nudges you when it is ready. I have, on occasion, come wide awake in the middle of the night and rushed to my desk to pour out flashes of inspiration.

Trying to make your brain work harder increases stress and further limits your ability to think. So when you're stuck, don't think too hard, quieten your mind, focus lightly on the issue and take in the relevant information, then take that break.

When the Plan Has To Change

I think we all accept that almost nothing goes exactly according to a plan. Sometimes this is used as an excuse not to plan. Imagine you were driving across the continent on a planned route and you came across an obstacle that blocked a part of the route. You would have to make an adjustment to the route and work around the obstacle. But you would still know what it would take to get back on the route. If you had no plan, you would not know which was the best way to get past the obstacle.

In the same way you will come across obstacles to any plan and you will have to make adjustments. Reworking a small part of the plan is still a lot simpler than randomly changing direction at every obstacle and hoping it gets you closer to your goal.

When you need to make a change, evaluate the obstacle, identify the effect on the overall plan and rework the part that is affected. Then update your calendar accordingly. If you have deadlines that cannot be missed for some reason (other than your own wishes) you may have to change some parts of the goal to ensure a successful outcome.

This is illustrated in a well-known project management model. The model illustrates three primary constraints; time, cost, and scope. Time is focused on a specific deadline. Cost focuses on the available resources, which could be money but in your case is probably your available hours. Scope is the activity and deliverables of the goal itself.

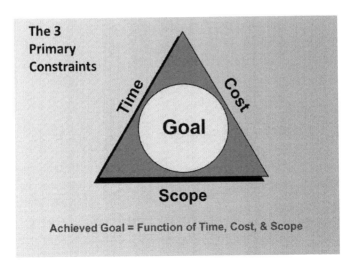

In any project, these three factors are likely to change. To keep the project in balance, if one changes, one or both of the others must be changed. Which one changes depends on the priorities amongst the three constraints.

If time (deadline) is the priority and something causes a delay, then you must apply more resources or drop some of the activities (scope), or some of both, to maintain the time constraint.

If resources are limited (your number of available hours) and something takes more hours than planned, then you must either accept an extended deadline or drop some of the activities (scope).

If the scope is the most important and you discover additional activities or components are necessary, you will have to apply more hours per day or extend the time, or some of both.

Here is a little exercise you can do to determine which constraints should change. In the table below put an X in the square to indicate your options.

- Constrain means it can't (or shouldn't) be changed
- Optimise means as good as possible
- Accept means whatever it takes

	Constrain (fixed)	Optimise (best possible)	Accept (floating)
Time			
Cost			
Scope			

For example, if I am writing a course for a client, I must identify which of the three constraints have the highest priority. Normally I can only choose one, sometimes two are possible, but never three. Then I will decide where the remaining one or two fit in the table.

The table below shows that the client had a fixed deadline to deliver the course on a specific date. Evaluation of the project determined that the content of the course should be as much of the topic as I could cover. This meant that the cost (hours worked) had to be floating. I would have to add whatever resources necessary to get the job done the way the client wanted it.

Course Design Project	Constrain (fixed)	Optimise (best possible)	Accept (floating)
Time	X		
Cost			X
Scope		X	

This exercise allows me to make the right decisions when an obstacle makes it necessary to change my plans.

Monitor Your Progress

Self-monitoring and seeking feedback are really important for successful outcomes on long-term activity.

When I am working on a long-term project, I sometimes find myself feeling the enormity of the task and a little intimidated. There are a number of ways I can deal with that.

First, I make sure the work is broken down into manageable chunks. Then I can simply take one small activity and treat that as a project on its own with a deadline. Therefore I can avoid thinking about all the rest while I am doing that.

When I reach the end of the activity I will stand back and look at the big picture again and cross off the completed work. The act of tracking and crossing off is usually a very effective way of keeping the mind in a positive mode. However, sometimes I feel bogged down, even on a small activity. In this case I find a way to break the remaining work into even smaller pieces and treat each item separately. Focusing on small activities makes it much easier to complete them, even when you don't like the task or you are finding it tedious.

Another trick I use when I am further along is to assemble the whole project and look at the incomplete parts or the gaps. Each activity to fill a gap then appears much smaller in the context of the whole. There is a powerful motivation when I can see how far I have come, and it gets me all fired up again to get at the unfinished parts.

A couple of warnings:

Make sure you celebrate the small achievements regularly. This provides positive reinforcement to your brain and helps maintain the positive mindset.
It's good to congratulate yourself on the intermediate successes, and to celebrate them. But be careful not to think that you have done so well you can relax. That is giving yourself permission to drop out for a while, and it can be very hard to get back at it. So as soon as you have celebrated, move your focus to what's next and what's left.

Missed deadlines can have a negative influence on your mindset. If it happens, understand if it was due to unforeseen issues. If so, recognise that you can't predict everything and it's ok to adjust your plan around the reality of life. If it was due to your own slacking off, then go back to your dream board and your goals and look for ways to re-motivate yourself or adjust your plans to something that works better for you.

Sometimes people can be over-optimistic when planning, and push themselves to disappointments when things don't work out. If it happens to you, then rethink your planning to accommodate the reality of your lifestyle.

Sometimes if people believe there is too little progress, they don't want to acknowledge it. So they put it off until the next checkpoint, when a better result is expected.

After You Get There

Reaching a goal is worthy of a celebration; it is a really good feeling. But the excitement does not last and there are often new problems with your new state.

When you reach a goal, you still need to retain discipline and commitment to stay there. You need to work at maintaining your position. The removal of past problems does not guarantee there will not be new problems.

If you have followed the path set out in this book and you have made positive lasting change to your habits and behaviour, you should have no problem continuing to grow and succeed.

Chapter 7: Putting it All Together
The Path to Success Model

The Path To Success Model

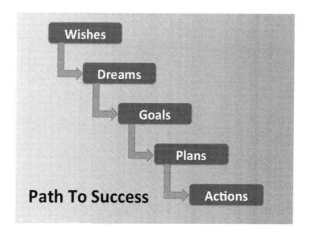

Step 1: Create your wish list

Make a list of your wishes, review the list and make sure that you really would like them to happen. Select those that are true.

Step 2: Turn your wishes into dreams

Identify the most important wishes, evaluate them and write down your dreams. This can be a single item or a list. You should not have more than 5 dreams on your list. If there is more than one, prioritise the list.

Step 3: Prioritise your dream list

Evaluate your long-term vision against your current needs and constraints, and rank the dreams by relative importance. Make sure you understand all the consequences of fulfilling those dreams, and that they are truly your desire.

Step 4: Develop your goals from your dreams

Taking one dream at a time, create a set of goals that are necessary to make the dream come true. Make sure the goals are S.M.A.R.T.

Step 5: Clearly define your goals

Take time to write out the goals very clearly so that you are able to identify all the work necessary to achieve the goal.

Step 6: Develop action plans from your goals

Build a set of plans that include long-term, high level deliverables, 2 to 5 or more years. Then build a medium-term plan for the current year. Finally a fully detailed plan for the next 90 days.

Step 7: Commit your plans to your calendar

Identify every activity necessary to complete your 90-day plan and find a place for it in your default calendar.

Step 8: Turn your plans into actions and get started

Use your default calendar to plan and execute each day in a reasonably controlled manner.

Step 9: Sustain the action

Continuously re-affirm, and re-plan as necessary. Keep your plans fresh and refreshed throughout the duration of your dream fulfillment.

Bonus Package

Download the bonus package to get a set of worksheets to help you through your goal-setting process. The package contains the following:

- Wish List Worksheet
- Dream List Worksheet
- The congruency test
- SMART worksheet
- Detailed Planning Worksheet
- 90 day planning Worksheet

Go to the website www.followthatdreambook.com for your package.

Made in the USA
Charleston, SC
29 January 2017